MOM,
WHAT'S YOUR
STORY?

A KEEPSAKE & GUIDED JOURNAL

FOR MOTHERS TO FILL IN AND GIVE BACK

INELL WILLIAMS

MOM,
WHAT'S YOUR
STORY?

A BOOK ABOUT:

_____ ,

MOTHER OF:

_____

_____

INTRODUCTION

This journal's prompts are divided into these main sections:

- *Time Capsule*
- *About Me*
- *I Prefer*
- *My Favorite*
- *Childhood*
- *Adulthood & Motherhood*
- *Fulfillment*
- *Customized Questions*

Attempt to answer the prompts honestly, and try not to overthink it. Taking a thorough and candid approach to your answers will help give future generations a more full, accurate picture of who you are as an individual.

Use specific names of people, brands, and places, as well as descriptive language (e.g. *a short boy wearing a red baseball cap; a narrow, bumpy road that always woke me up as we drove on it*) to paint a more detailed, vivid picture of you and the world you inhabit.

For the prompts with checkboxes, feel free to select several answers if you feel that more than one applies to you.

And most importantly, have fun sharing your story!

TIME CAPSULE

Today's date: _____

THE CURRENT PRICE OF

Eggs, 1 dozen:	Milk, 1 gallon:
Gas, unleaded regular, 1 gallon:	Coffee, 1 cup:
Plane ticket from _____ to _____ :	White bread, 1 loaf:
_____ :	_____ :

These are prices for (City/ Town): _____

(Province/ State/ Region): _____   (Country): _____

At least one significant worldly event that has occurred within the past year:

_____

_____

Two significant events that have occurred in black culture, entertainment or politics within the past year, one negative and one positive:

_____

_____

A current trend in fashion: _____

A current trend on social media: _____

The leader of my country is now: _____

The population size of my country is now: _____

The world population is now: _____

One large news story that broke out recently:

_____

One most-talked-about advancement in science or technology recently:

_____

An interesting recent breakthrough in medicine:

_____

A song that is currently very popular:

_____

A TV show that is currently popular:

_____

A current serious crisis in another country:

_____

A PICTURE OF ME NOW

— ABOUT ME —

Name:	Date of birth:
Born in:	Height:
Hair color:	Hair texture:
Eye color:	Eye shape:

Traits and features I'm known most for:

_____

My clothing style is

_____

Jewelry and/ or accessories that I wear often include

_____

_____

Western/ Chinese zodiacs & Greek temperament (Are they accurate for me?):

_____

I took a personality quiz. My personality type is: _____

I took the political compass test. My politics are: _____

I PREFER

☐ heels ☐ being barefoot

☐ sandals

☐ sneakers ☐ _____

☐ city (urban)

☐ country (rural)

☐ dogs ☐ cats

☐ both

☐ neither

☐ _____

☐ no makeup ☐ natural makeup

☐ full glam ☐ something in between natural and full glam

☐ _____

☐ staying in ☐ going out

Pineapple on pizza is...

☐ delicious, om nom nom.

☐ an abomination.

☐ Never tried it, but I'm interested in trying.

☐ Never tried it, and not interested in trying.

Hooking up:

☐ I'm all for free love.

☐ It's fine. There's a limit, but I live and let live.

☐ It's bad.

☐ _____

Eating insects:

☐ Yum!

☐ Can't be too bad. Would try.

☐ Maybe I'd try it, begrudingly, to be open-minded.

☐ Hell no!

My steak: ☐ better be well-done. ☐ medium ☐ bloody ☐ _____

- ☐ loud music
- ☐ soft music
- ☐ it depends

- ☐ to be underdressed
- ☐ to be overdressed

Eggs

- ☐ soft-boiled
- ☐ hard-boiled
- ☐ Who eats soft-boiled eggs??
- ☐ _____

- ☐ low maintenance
- ☐ high maintenance

- ☐ left-wing
- ☐ right-wing
- ☐ it depends
- ☐ don't care
- ☐ it's all the same
- ☐ _____

- ☐ sweet
- ☐ savory
- ☐ _____

Colors (clothing)

- ☐ bright ☐ muted ☐ solid
- ☐ bold/ busy prints ☐ minimalist prints

- ☐ natural hair
- ☐ wigs
- ☐ relaxed hair
- ☐ weaves
- ☐ flat-ironed hair
- ☐ braids/ twists
- ☐ locs
- ☐ updos
- ☐ short
- ☐ medium ☐ natural color
- ☐ long ☐ bold color
- ☐ _____

When I'm planning/ working on something

- ☐ everyone will know about it.
- ☐ a few close people will know.
- ☐ others might hear about it sooner or later. Unbothered either way.
- ☐ that's my business. I move in silence.

Femininity:

- ☐ important for all women
- ☐ beautiful but to each their own
- ☐ unimportant to me
- ☐ screw gender roles

— MY FAVORITE —

Color:	Food:
Music genre(s):	Book genre(s):
Movie genre(s):	Activity:
Perfume:	Season of the year:
Game(s):	Way to unwind:
Place to travel:	Holiday:

This is my favorite book, movie, and song:

They're my favorite because

MORE OF MY FAVORITES

Podcast:	Show/ channel:
----------------------- :	----------------------- :
----------------------- :	----------------------- :
----------------------- :	----------------------- :

"There was a time when

meadow, grove, and stream,

The earth, and every common sight,

To me did seem

Apparell'd in celestial light,

The glory and the freshness

of a dream...."

— William Wordsworth,

Ode (Recollections of Early Childhood)

CHILDHOOD
&
ADOLESCENCE

ME AS A YOUNG CHILD

As a young child my personality was _____

_____

I liked _____ music. Some of my favorite shows to watch were:

_____

_____

_____

Some of my hobbies and interests included:

_____

_____

_____

_____

I was friends with:

_____

_____

My pets were:

_____

_____

My earliest memory was:

_____

_____

As a young child, I remember being punished/ scolded for:

_____

_____

_____

_____

_____

_____

_____

_____

I remember being praised for:

_____

_____

_____

_____

_____

_____

_____

_____

I grew up in _____

I felt that this location was

☐ a nice place.   ☐ not a very nice place.   ☐ just meh.   ☐ ... it's
                                                                complicated.

Why I feel this way:

_____

_____

_____

_____

Some memories I have about this place:

_____

_____

_____

_____

_____

_____

_____

_____

_____

ME AS A TEENAGER

As a teenager my personality was _____

_____

I liked _____ music. Some of my favorite shows to watch were:

_____

_____

_____

Some of my hobbies and interests included:

_____

_____

_____

_____

I was friends with:

_____

_____

My pets were:

_____

_____

At this time I had a pet peeve about:

_____

_____

As a teenager, I remember being punished/ scolded for:

_____

_____

_____

_____

_____

_____

_____

I remember being praised for:

_____

_____

_____

_____

_____

_____

_____

_____

As a teenager I struggled with:

_____

_____

_____

_____

_____

_____

_____

As a teenager I took pride in:

_____

_____

_____

_____

_____

_____

_____

The schools I attended were _____

_____

_____

School was

☐ great!   ☐ torture.   ☐ a'ight.   ☐ boring.   ☐ engaging.

I was a _____ student.

Some of my favorite teachers and subjects were:

_____

_____

_____

_____

Some of my memories and thoughts about school and education in general:

_____

_____

_____

_____

_____

_____

_____

_____

Growing up, the cousins/ family members whom I spent the most time with were _____

_____

_____

Some stories about my family members:

_____

_____

_____

_____

_____

_____

_____

_____

_____

_____

_____

_____

_____

_____

A very happy memory from my childhood or adolescence:

A few funny or interesting stories from childhood/ adolescence:

Here are some of my memories about holidays as a child/ teenager:

_____

_____

_____

_____

_____

_____

_____

_____

_____

_____

_____

_____

_____

_____

_____

_____

_____

_____

My parents were...

_____

_____

_____

_____

_____

_____

_____

_____

_____

_____

_____

_____

_____

_____

_____

My mother's family was...

_____

_____

_____

_____

_____

_____

_____

_____

_____

_____

_____

_____

_____

_____

_____

My father's family was...

Revisit William Wordsworth's poem excerpt at the beginning of this section. Some mundane childhood memories (e.g. common sights, smells, experiences, daily routines, random people that still stand out in memory, etc.) that I would like to put down on paper, so I don't forget:

"Blessings on the hand of women!

Angels guard its strength and grace.

In the palace, cottage, hovel,

Oh, no matter where the place;

Would that never storms assailed it,

Rainbows ever gently curled;

For the hand that rocks the cradle

Is the hand that rules the world."

— William Ross Wallace,

The Hand That Rocks The Cradle

ADULTHOOD
&
MOTHERHOOD

ME AND MY CHILD(REN)

As an adult my personality is _____

_____

I like _____ music. Some of my favorite shows to watch are:

_____

_____

_____

Some of my hobbies and interests include:

_____

_____

_____

_____

I am friends with:

_____

_____

My pets are:

_____

_____

Some fun facts about me:

_____

_____

Some of my favorite public figures (e.g. celebrities, politicians, spiritual figures, scientists, etc.) are:

_____

_____

_____

I'm fond of them because:

_____

_____

_____

_____

_____

_____

_____

_____

_____

_____

_____

_____

One positive and important thing I've learned about friendship as an adult is:

_____

_____

_____

_____

_____

_____

_____

One negative and important thing I've learned about friendship as an adult is:

_____

_____

_____

_____

_____

_____

_____

_____

Here are some interesting dreams I had that I remember:

When I was young, I felt that being black is _____

_____

_____

As I've gotten older, my feelings have   ☐ changed.   ☐ stayed the same.

More of my thoughts about my experience as a black person, and the black experience in general:

_____

_____

_____

_____

_____

_____

_____

_____

_____

_____

_____

What I felt when I learned that I was pregnant with my child(ren):

Some memories I have of my child(ren) when they were a baby:

My favorite children's books, toys, games, and gifts that I gave my child(ren) were:

_____

_____

_____

_____

_____

_____

_____

_____

_____

_____

_____

_____

_____

_____

_____

_____

The story of how I met

☐ your father: ☐ my partner: ☐ _____

_____

_____

_____

_____

_____

_____

_____

_____

_____

_____

_____

_____

_____

_____

_____

Generally, my beliefs, values and worldviews from adolescence to adulthood have ☐ changed. ☐ stayed the same.

For example:

_____

_____

_____

_____

_____

_____

_____

_____

_____

_____

_____

_____

_____

_____

As I answer this prompt, I am _____ years old. Even so, I feel:

☐ younger.   ☐ like my age.   ☐ older.   ☐ that it's rude to ask a
                                                            woman her age.

I think this is because:

_____

_____

_____

_____

_____

_____

_____

_____

_____

_____

_____

_____

_____

_____

Some positive ways that the world has changed since I was younger:

_____

_____

_____

_____

_____

_____

_____

_____

Some negative ways that the world has changed since I was younger:

_____

_____

_____

_____

_____

_____

_____

_____

Some of the most difficult things about being an adult are:

_____

_____

_____

_____

_____

_____

_____

Some of the most rewarding things about being an adult are:

_____

_____

_____

_____

_____

_____

_____

Some of the most difficult things about being a mother are:

_____

_____

_____

_____

_____

_____

_____

_____

Some of the most rewarding things about being a mother are:

_____

_____

_____

_____

_____

_____

_____

_____

Some of the challenges of black motherhood that I or the moms around me have experienced are:

_____

_____

_____

_____

_____

_____

Some of the rewards of black motherhood that I or the moms around me have experienced are:

_____

_____

_____

_____

_____

_____

_____

What I'd like my daughter(s) or son(s) to know about my experience as a black mom:

_____
_____
_____
_____
_____
_____
_____
_____
_____
_____
_____
_____
_____
_____

To laugh often and much;

To win the respect of intelligent people

and the affection of children;

To earn the appreciation of honest critics

and endure the betrayal of false friends;

To appreciate beauty;

To find the best in others;

To leave the world a bit better,

whether by a healthy child, a garden patch

or a redeemed social condition;

To know even one life has breathed easier

because you have lived;

This is to have succeeded.

— Ralph Waldo Emerson,
To Laugh Often and Much

FULFILLMENT

When I was a child, I wanted to be _____

when I grew up. When I got older, I became _____

_____

Some thoughts and memories about my life's work so far

(e.g. career, jobs, volunteering, homemaking, caretaking, charity, education,

certifications, etc.)

_____

_____

_____

_____

_____

_____

_____

_____

_____

_____

_____

_____

_____

About my firsts (e.g. first job, kiss, first time living alone, first plane ride, etc.)

When I was a child, my relationship with spirituality/ religion was

_____

_____

_____

_____

My current relationship with spirituality/ religion is _____

_____

_____

_____

_____

_____

_____

_____

_____

In the future, in regards to my spirituality/ religion, I hope that

_____

_____

_____

_____

Some goals that I have right now include (e.g. productivity, friendships, relationships, health, self-growth, travel, etc.):

_____

_____

_____

_____

_____

_____

_____

_____

_____

_____

_____

Where I see myself in five to ten years:

_____

_____

_____

_____

Some things that I've learned about self-care and happiness are:

_____

_____

_____

_____

_____

_____

_____

_____

_____

_____

_____

_____

_____

_____

_____

_____

A few of my regrets that I want my children to learn from:

The best day of my life so far was:

_____

_____

_____

_____

_____

_____

_____

_____

_____

_____

_____

_____

_____

_____

_____

_____

_____

Some events or milestones that I'm looking forward to as I get older are:

I want my grandchildren, great-grandchildren and so on to know that...

_____

_____

_____

_____

_____

_____

_____

_____

_____

_____

_____

_____

_____

_____

_____

_____

_____

CUSTOMIZED
QUESTIONS

Specific question(s) about my childhood and adolescence that my child(ren) can ask me here:

_____

_____

_____

_____

_____

_____

_____

My answer(s):

_____

_____

_____

_____

_____

_____

_____

_____

_____

_____

Specific question(s) about my experience with motherhood and adulthood that my child(ren) can ask me here:

My answer(s):

_____

_____

_____

_____

_____

_____

_____

_____

_____

Specific question(s) about fulfillment that my child(ren) can ask me here:

My answer(s):

More questions to me from my child(ren):

My answers:

Glue four mementos of me here (e.g. a lock of hair,
a piece of a scarf, a cutout of a birthday card, etc.)

Made in the USA
Las Vegas, NV
06 May 2025

21816104R00057